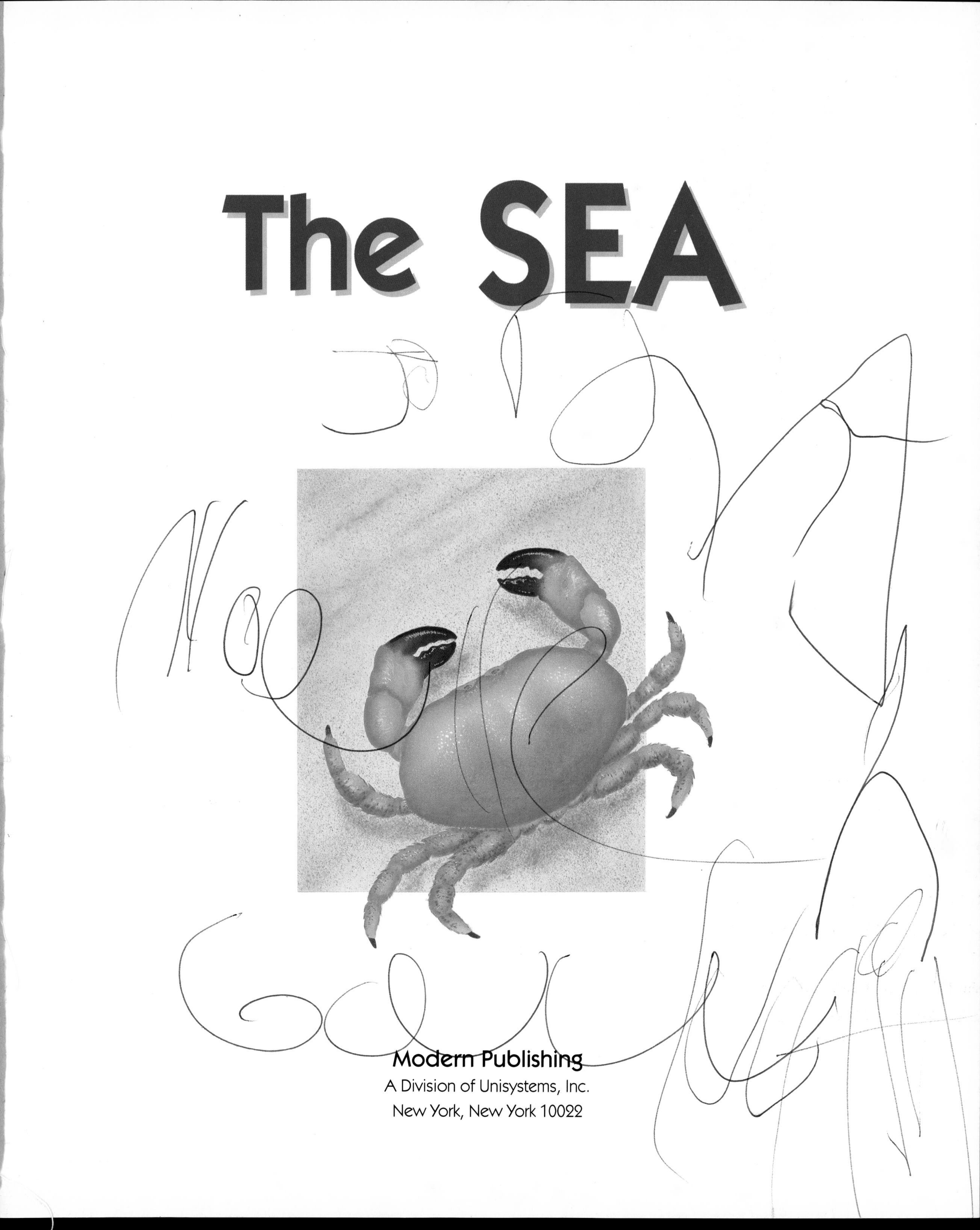

The SEA

Modern Publishing
A Division of Unisystems, Inc.
New York, New York 10022

CONTENTS

Under the Waves

A Different Experience—The environment under water is different from the one we know on land. To explore it you must enter a new dimension. The sunlight barely filters through from above, and sounds are muffled. The plants and animals that live in the sea are very different from those on land.

Observing the Sea

Swimming—There are many ways to look at the sea: lying on the sand under an umbrella, or maybe sitting in a boat. The best way to discover the secrets of the sea, though, is to go snorkeling or deep-sea diving.

Looking Under Water— Snorkeling goggles fit snugly against your face so that water can't get into your nose.
The rubber tube that sticks up out of the water allows you to breathe while you are underwater. If water gets into the tube, all you have to do is blow hard and the water will come out in a spurt.

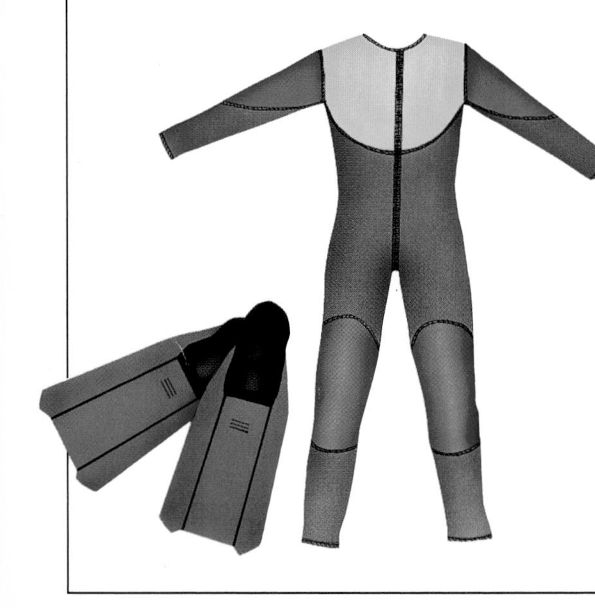

Fins and wet suit

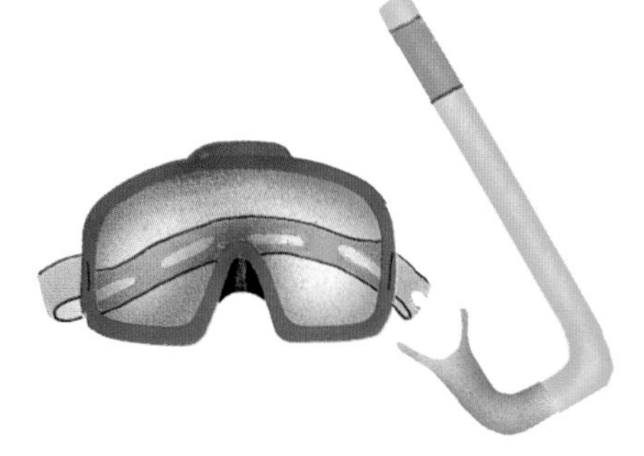

Goggles and snorkel

Fins—Although we call them "fins," they are much more like a duck's webbed feet. They help you swim fast and can save your energy.

Oxygen Tanks—The air contained in oxygen diving tanks lets swimmers stay underwater for a long time. Diving with oxygen tanks is not easy and can be dangerous, so divers must know how to use them properly. It is important to know how to come up from deep water. Rising too quickly doesn't allow your body to adjust to the changes in water pressure and can cause severe damage to your body.

A Fish's Life

Everyone Has a Place— There are animals that love the desert heat, and others that prefer the ice. In the sea, too, there are different habitats suitable for some kinds of fish, but not others. Although fish swim freely in the water, they all live in an environment that is most suitable for their needs. Some live at the bottom of the sea.

Those that feed on algae live near the surface of the water because these plants cannot grow deep down, where there is no light.

An Important Sensor— How can fish tell what is around them in the water? First of all they can see, but fish have another important sense. Fish have "lateral lines," sensors along each side of their bodies. From these sensors a fish can get information about water pressure and currents.

Swimming Like a Fish—Fish have a soft sack called an "air bladder" that helps to keep them afloat. This sack deflates when they want to go down deeper in the water and inflates when they come up. If a deep-water fish is suddenly brought up to the surface, the air bladder inflates and suffocates the fish.

Staying Afloat—Sharks don't have air bladders, so if they stopped swimming they would sink. To stay afloat sharks swim all the time, even when they are asleep.

Breathing Like a Fish—Fish don't have lungs. Instead they have gills. When a fish breathes, it takes in water through its mouth. The water then passes through the fish's gills, where oxygen is absorbed from it into the fish's blood.

Fish Behind Glass—In aquariums you can observe all kinds of creatures that live in water: sharks, turtles, tropical fish, octopuses, and seals, as well as ordinary fish like mackerel or sole.

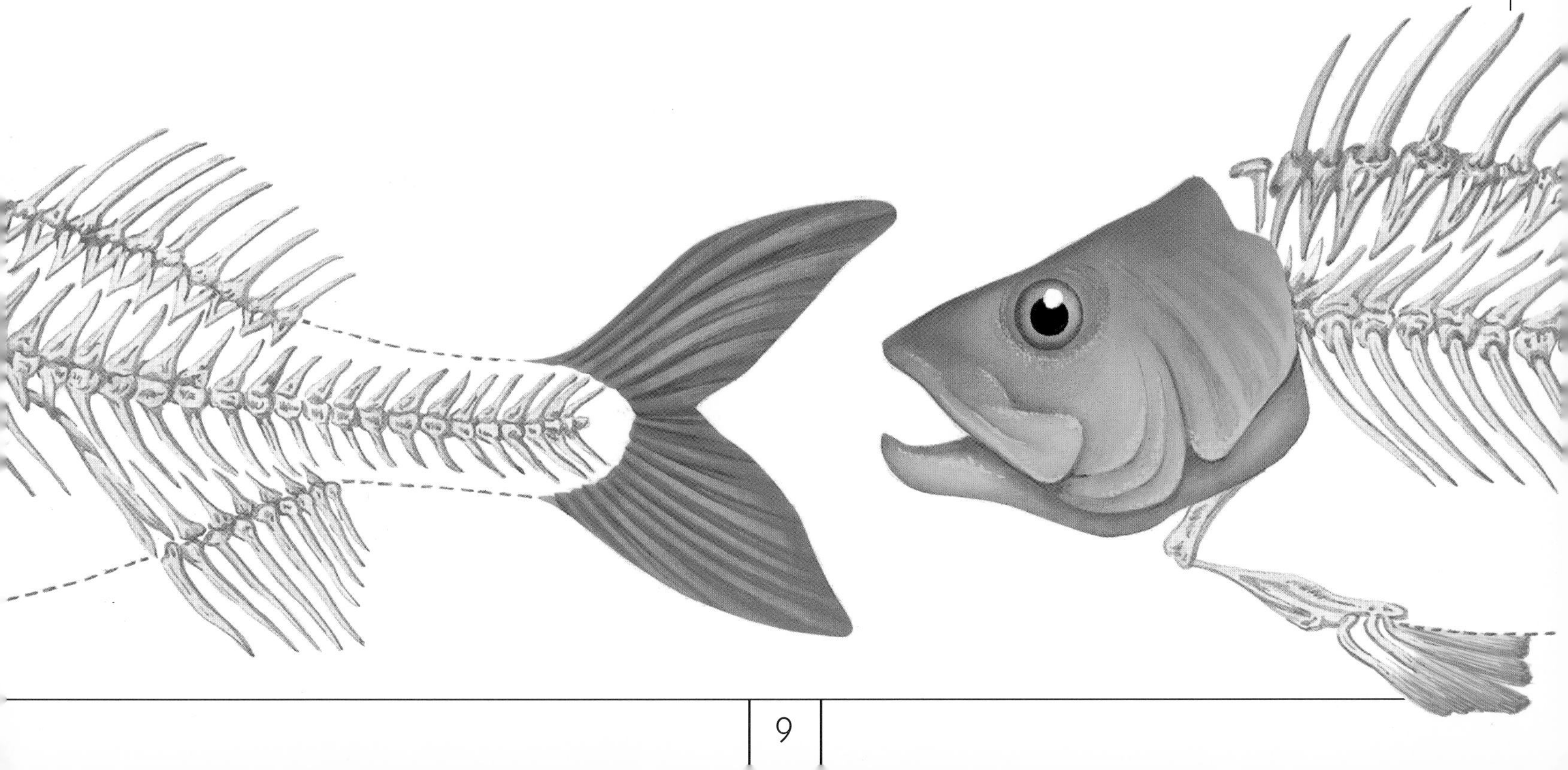

The Strangest Fish

Beware of the Shark—Most people feel afraid when they see a shark fin moving quickly through the water. Sharks' teeth are very sharp and pointed. Their mouths open very, very wide so they can easily swallow their prey. Sharks often follow in a ship's wake, eating anything that is thrown overboard. The most dangerous sharks are the white mako shark, the tiger shark, and the blue shark.

Friends—The pilot fish and remoras swim with sharks and never leave them. People used to think that sharks were blind and were guided

Sharks are ancient fish, almost like dinosaurs. Their skeletons are made of cartilage, not bone.

by the pilot fish and remoras. Today we know that these fish travel with the sharks because there is always an abundant food supply around them.

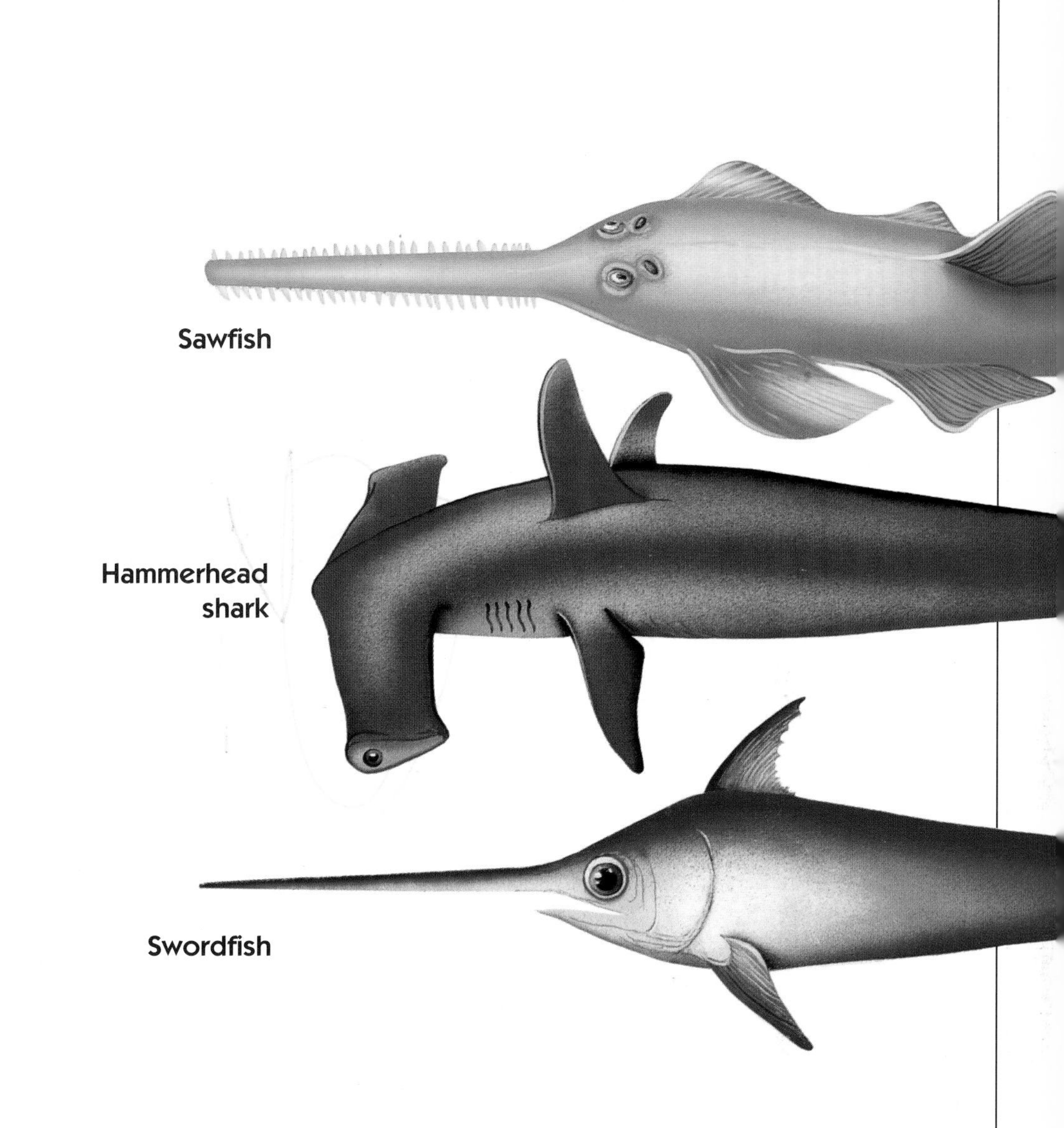

Fish with Strange Noses— The sawfish has a long nose with teeth like a saw. The hammerhead shark has eyes that sprout from its hammer-shaped snout. The swordfish's snout is shaped like a long pointed sword.

The flying scorpion fish has fins that almost look like birds' wings.

Other Strange Fish—The seahorse is the strangest of all sea creatures. It has a head like a horse, but a body like an upside down question mark. The manta ray has fins that open and close like giant wings.

Some Fly, Some Glow— Flying fish sometimes shoot so high out of the sea that they land on a boat or a bridge. Some fish that live in the deepest and darkest parts of the ocean are luminescent—they glow in the dark.

Small Fish

Advantages—Being big is not always an advantage. Small fish, for example, can hide between algae and reefs more easily than larger fish.

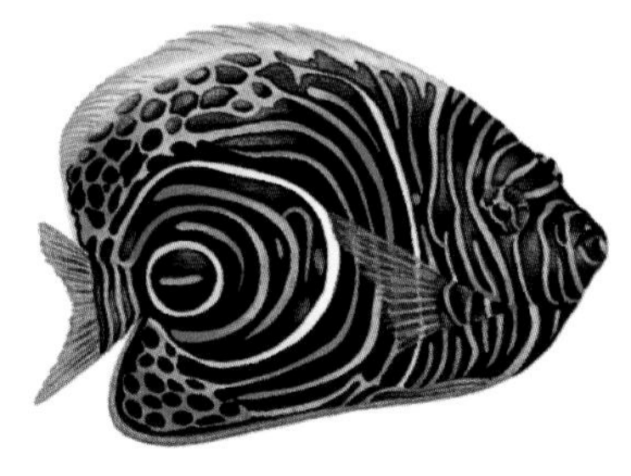

Young angel fish

Red Mullet—This is a bright red fish that is found in the Mediterranean Sea. It has two whiskers called "barbels" that it uses to explore the sandy sea floor in search of food.

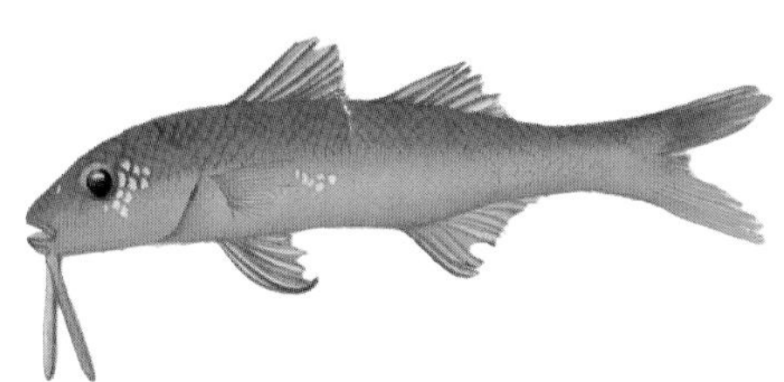

Red mullet

Packed Like Sardines—Sardines constantly swim about in large groups, called "schools." Sardines are a very popular food and are caught in great numbers. They are eaten by other fish as well as by humans.

School of sardines

Clown Fish—These are orange fish with vertical yellow and white stripes that almost look as if they have been painted on. Clown fish live among the actiniae (a type of sea anemone that has poisonous tentacles), but the clown fish are immune to their poison.

Clown fish

Small and Fancy—In the ocean, where there is light you can see colors. You can admire the brilliant colors of the small fish that live in shallow waters and in the great coral reefs. They have multicolored tails, striped or polka-dotted

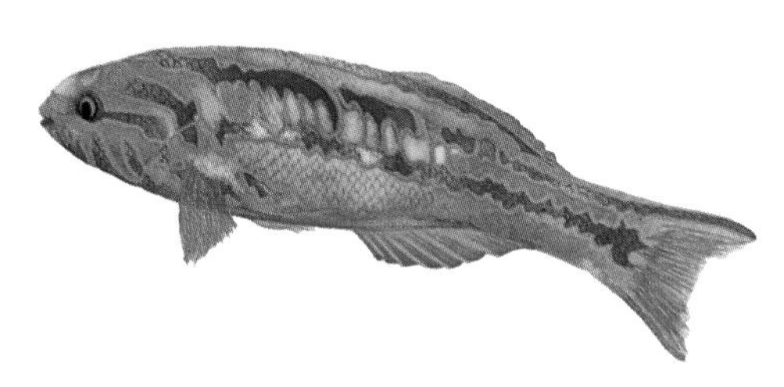

Rainbow parrot fish

bodies of all colors, and some are even fluorescent. Some fish can change from one color to another and then change back again. Why? Fish cannot bark or growl, twitter or

Blenny

Blenny—This creature has the strange habit of leaving the water and lying on top of reefs. It just needs occasional splashes of water in order to breathe.

Adult angel fish

roar. So they communicate with color. The colored stripes, multi-hued tails and eyes usually are signs to their enemies to stay away. As you go farther away from the light, little by little you see less color and the fish are less colorful.

Algae

Very, Very Old—Sea plants are very ancient. Because algae float in the water, they do not need sturdy stems to support them the way land plants do. But like all plants, they do need sunlight. This is why algae are found on or near the surface of seawater. They can't live deep down in the sea, where the sunlight never reaches.

Algae Can Be Eaten—Seaweed can be eaten. There are delicious Japanese dishes based on seaweed. These foods have become popular all over the world. Some kinds of seaweed are used to make gelatin and many medicines.

Here is a type of delicious Japanese food called "sushi." Each piece of sushi has a different filling, but each one is wrapped in seaweed. Some have a piece of raw fish or seafood in them.

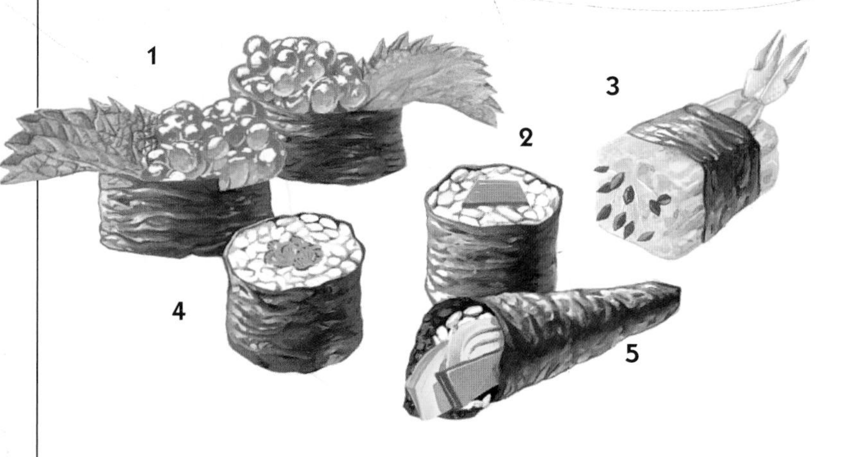

1. Steamed rice and fish eggs
2. Steamed rice and raw tuna
3. Steamed bean curd and shrimp
4. Steamed rice and vegetables
5. Steamed rice, raw fish, and avocado

Very, Very Small—Some seaweeds grow on rocks or reefs; others just float, carried by the current, not attached to anything. Seaweeds come in all sizes, some so small they can be seen only by using a microscope.

An Underwater Garden—There are seaweeds of every shape and color. In some parts of the ocean, where the current is not very strong, seaweed will grow to be hundreds of feet long. There is a kind of seaweed called "sargasso" that is so abundant, the sea in which it grows has been named the Sargasso Sea.

Flowers and Fruits of the Sea—There are seaweeds that have roots, flowers, and fruit—just like plants that live on land. In the Mediterranean Sea there is a type of seaweed called "posidonian" that covers the sea floor. In autumn it flowers and bears fruit. In Greek mythology Poseidon was the god of the sea.

There are many kinds and colors of algae.

Salt from the Sea

After the seawater evaporates salt crystals remain.

Precious—Seawater tastes of salt and it can irritate your eyes. This is because there is a lot of salt in the sea. Salt is one of the most precious treasures we get from the sea. It is important for our health and it also improves the taste of the food we eat. In ancient times salt was considered so precious that some people used it as currency for trading. In Europe the salt dish was always placed in front of honored guests at dinner. Today there is still the superstition that spilling salt is unlucky. This is because when salt was rare, to spill it was to waste it.

Why is the Sea Salty?— One pint of salt water contains approximately two teaspoons of salt. Among the salts that we find dissolved in seawater today are some that were on the surface of the land when it was covered by water many years ago. Other salts are carried to the sea by rivers. Underwater volcanic eruptions also add salts from inside the earth to the sea.

Magical Dust—Salt has more uses than just making our food taste good. It is used to preserve food and is used by industry to produce medicines, acids, and colorings. It can also be used to melt ice. This is because salty water freezes at a lower temperature than fresh water.

Salterns—Salt is separated from sea-water in salterns—long shallow vats that are dug along the coastlines in warm climates. The seawater evaporates from the vats and the salt crystals that remain are collected and refined for use.

It is easier to float in the sea than in fresh-water lakes or pools.

Salt sticks together in lumps
when the weather is humid.
To prevent this put a few grains
of rice in the salt shaker.

Danger in the Sea

Swallowed Up by the Sea—Whirlpools are very strong circular currents that suck water downward to the depths of the ocean. The most fearsome are those along the Norwegian coasts, called Maelstrom's Vortices, which are capable of swallowing up large ships.

Little Water—Shallow water can be very dangerous. Ships can run aground on sandbanks or get stuck on rocks or reefs. Fortunately, the oceans' depths are indicated on nautical maps. These maps show the depth of the sea and coasts mile by mile and where there are rocks, sandbanks, and reefs.

Other Dangers—Sometimes unusually large waves form. These can be very dangerous. Today, with satellite communications, it is possible for sailors to be warned in time. Weather satellites can also warn ships when hurricanes, tornadoes, or tidal waves might cross their path.

Floating Mountains—Everyone who travels in the polar seas sooner or later sees great floating mountains of ice, called "icebergs," that are carried by the ocean currents. Where do they come from? Icebergs are enormous pieces of ice that break off from the polar ice-pack, the icy crust that is found around the North and South Poles, and float away.

Above and Below—As big as these icebergs look, sailors know that only about one-seventh of the iceberg shows above water. The real danger of icebergs is beneath the waves. This is why ships are very careful to avoid them.

Avoiding Disaster—In the past many ships sank after crashing into an iceberg. In 1912 the luxury ocean liner the *Titanic* sank after hitting an iceberg. Today, such danger is diminished because ships are equipped with radar and sonar devices. Satellites are used to warn ships when icebergs are near. There is even an international ice patrol that follows the movements of icebergs and continually warns ships when icebergs are near.

Icebergs can have different shapes: those from the North Pole look like polished mountains, while those from the South Pole look like large platforms.

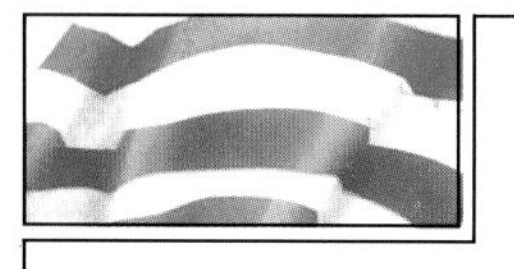

Coded Signals

Speaking from Far Away—Today all ships are equipped with radios that are used by sailors to communicate with other ships at sea and with ports around the world. Before radio was invented the only way sailors could communicate with each other was with flashing light signals and flags of different colors and designs hung from a ship's riggings. Although ships commonly use radio to communicate today, flashing lights, flags, and signal buoys are still used. Flags represent letters, numbers, and even whole messages. When a ship is about to sail from port it flies a flag called a "Blue Peter," a square blue flag with a white square in the middle.

S. O. S.—"Mayday. Mayday!" A ship that sends that radio message is in trouble. "Mayday" comes from the French "M'aidez," which means "help me." The letters "S. O. S." are the initials of the message "Save our souls."

R—Signal my distance.
K—I ask for communication.
O—Man overboard.
U—Danger in front of you.
G—Pilot needed.
T—Ships fishing in pairs.
I—Close to port.

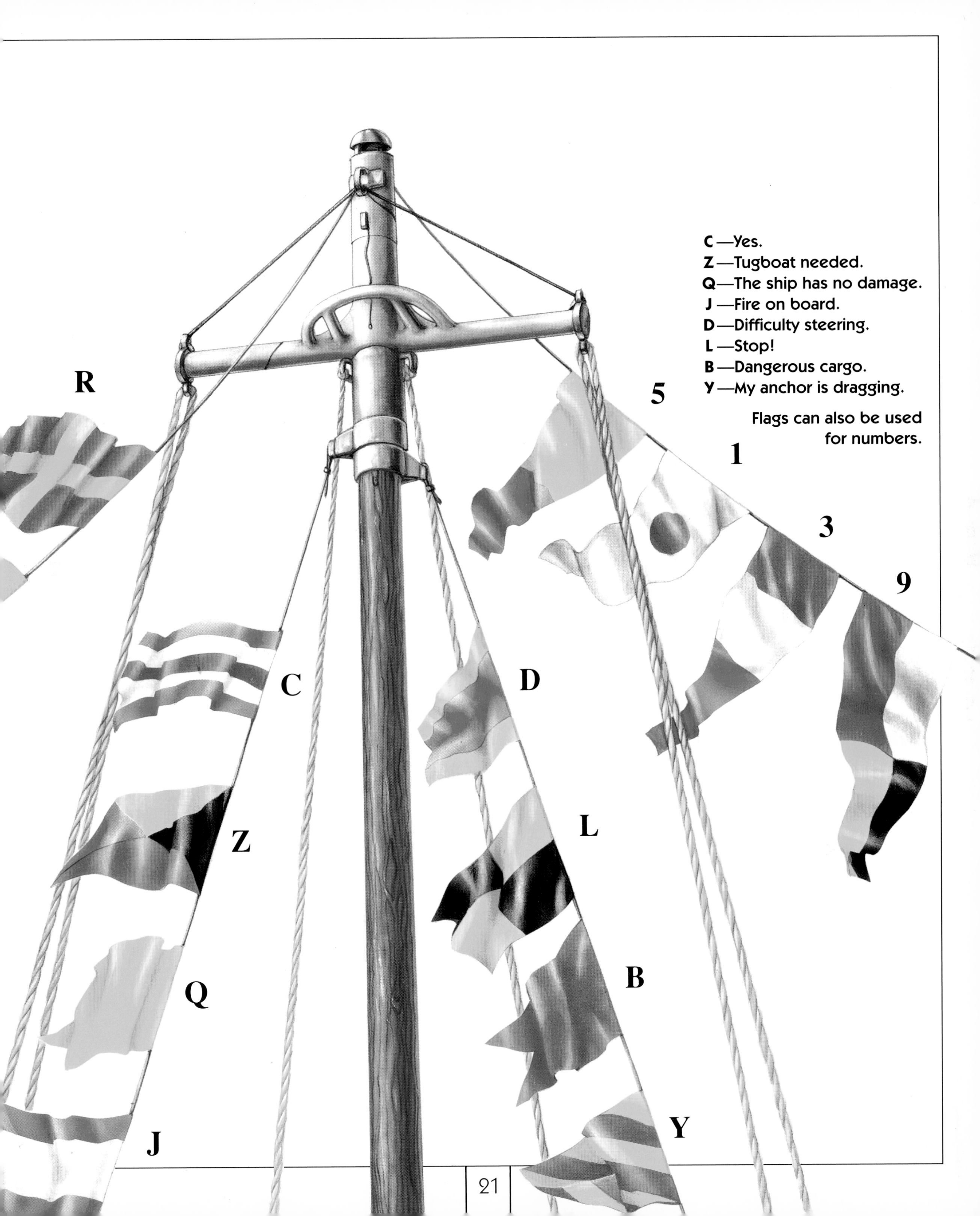

C —Yes.
Z —Tugboat needed.
Q —The ship has no damage.
J —Fire on board.
D —Difficulty steering.
L —Stop!
B —Dangerous cargo.
Y —My anchor is dragging.

Flags can also be used for numbers.

From Octopus to Jellyfish

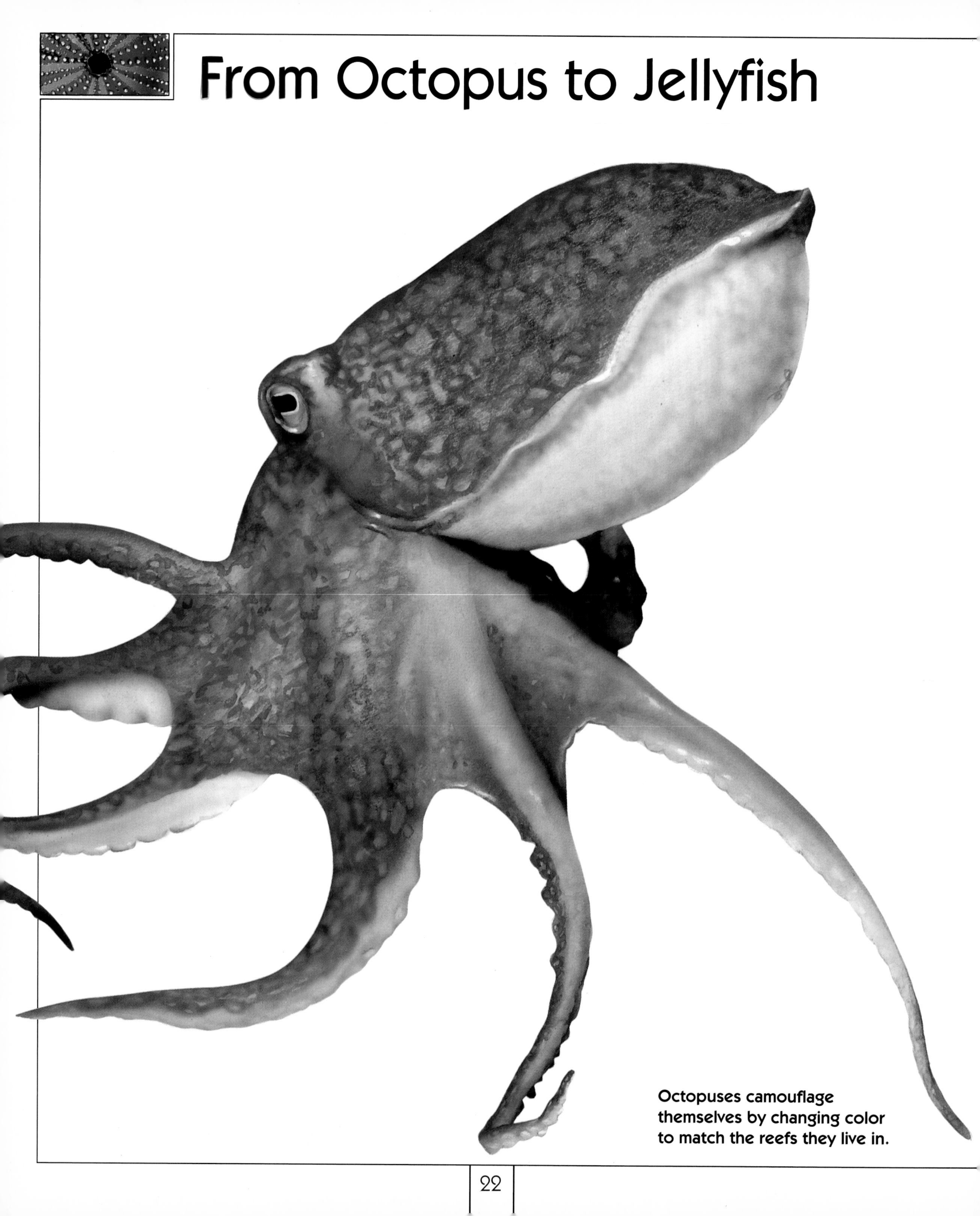

Octopuses camouflage themselves by changing color to match the reefs they live in.

Jellyfish are mostly water. They melt in the sun.

Jellyfish—They look like gelatin, but it's best to leave them alone, because when they are touched they emit a substance that will make your skin sting. Some jellyfish light up in the dark.

Long Tentacles—Octopuses are very intelligent animals. They have eight long tentacles covered with suckers that can grip things. They can use their tentacles like arms. When waiting for prey, they hide in coral reefs and change color to match the reefs. They become red in red coral, brown in brown coral, and in seaweed they turn green. They are very curious and will go to investigate anything that attracts them. When they are frightened or hunted, octopuses squirt a black liquid in which to hide.

Sea Urchins—Watch where you walk! If you step on a sea urchin, your foot will be covered with painful spines.

Flower or Animal?—Sea anemones look like colorful flowers, but they are animals that live on the ocean floor firmly attached to rocks. They defend themselves from their enemies, such as jellyfish, with poisonous tentacles.

Starfish—The starfish is one of the most voracious creatures in the sea. Not even a closely shut oyster shell can stop it when it is hungry. The starfish holds the oyster in a vicelike grip until the shell is forced open.

Sea urchin shells come in many colors and each one is different.

The Future of the Sea

Treasure Island—For hundreds of years people have dreamed of finding treasure at the bottom of the sea. Now we have begun to realize that the most precious treasure is a clean ocean, populated by seaweed, healthy fish, and other marine creatures.

A Garbage Can—For years people have treated the ocean like a garbage dump. It is able to break down a lot of trash, but now many parts of the sea are very polluted and we can no longer use the sea as a trash can.

Eliminating the Trash—Certain materials, such as leaves that fall from trees, are easily broken down by the sea. Others, like waste water, require great quantities of oxygen to clean. This takes oxygen away from sea plants, fish, and other sea creatures. Substances like oil and plastic cannot be absorbed by the sea.

Future or Science Fiction—There are already too many people on earth and people are always looking for new places to live. Airports that are entirely on water are already in existence, and many islands are connected to the mainland by underwater tunnels. Maybe in the future there will be artificial islands or underwater cities, but at the moment this is just science fiction.

Come See the Ocean

The cuttlefish hides from its enemies in a cloud of ink.

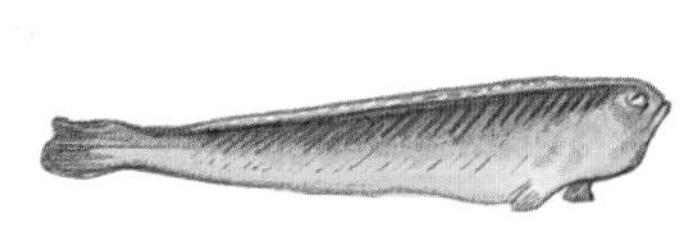

The lamprey eats by attaching itself to the flesh of its prey.

Sea snails look like land snails.

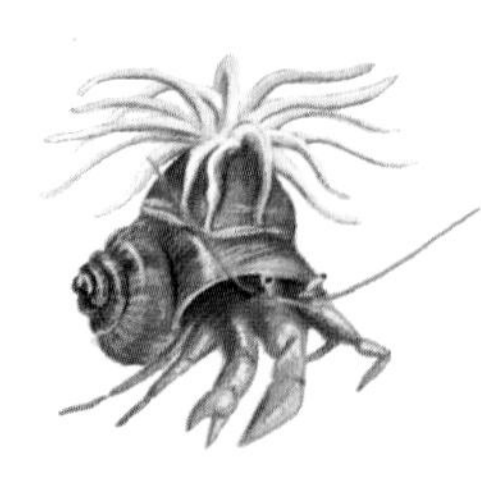

The hermit crab moves to a new shell as its old one becomes too small.

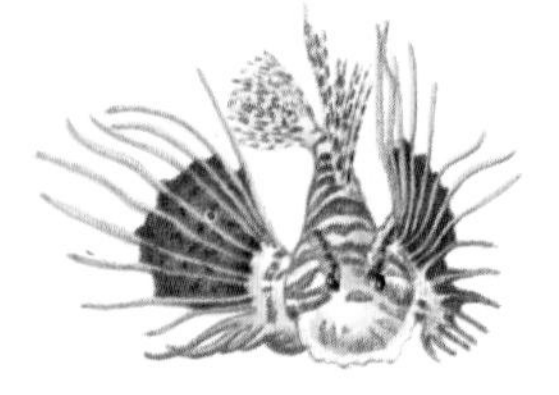

The lion fish has large side fins that look like fans.

The seahorse has a head that looks like a horse, and a curling body.

The skate is dangerous. Beware of its poisonous tail spike.

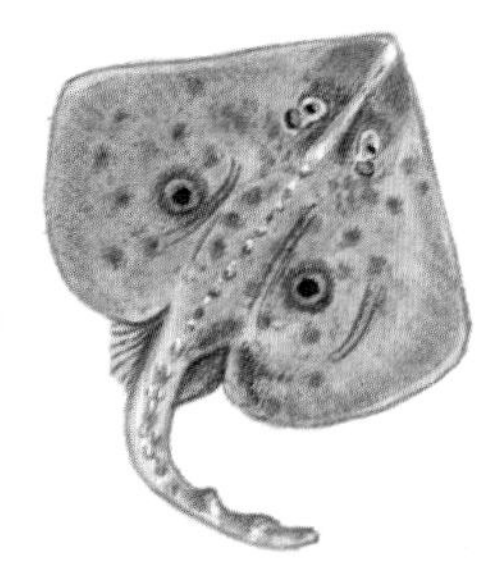

The sole is a flat fish that hides in the sand at the sea bottom.

The cowrie is as shiny as porcelain.

Squid come in all sizes.

The nudibranch is a mollusk without a shell.

Some sea anemones look like flowers but are really animals.

Open and look for . . .

The parrot fish is more colorful than a real parrot.

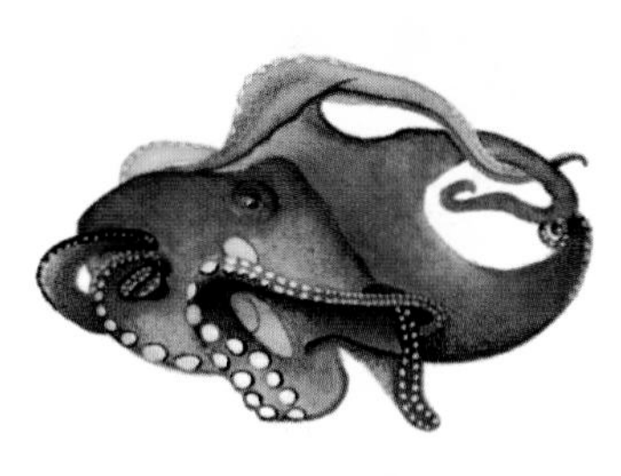

The octopus has eight tentacles covered with suction cups.

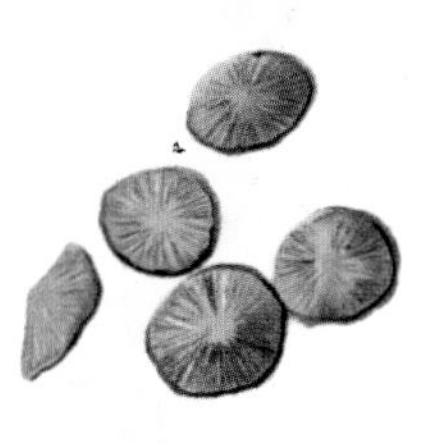

Limpets attach themselves firmly to rocks and reefs.

Barnacles attach themselves to anything they can—rocks, ships, docks.

Sea urchins have very sharp spines.

Lobsters can grow to be about 10 inches long.

Mussels have beautiful black shells.

Coral is formed by many small polyps. Starfish eat the polyps.

Some eels can give shocks under water.

Sea anemones have poisonous tentacles.

The clown fish is striped like a clown's costume.

The grouper has a large mouth filled with teeth.

. . . a small sea snail.

S.O.S. from the Sea

When you see a plastic bottle or
soft-drink can floating in the ocean,
it is a sign that the sea needs help.
Don't throw trash in the water
when you go to the beach. We
and many other creatures depend
on clean water to survive.

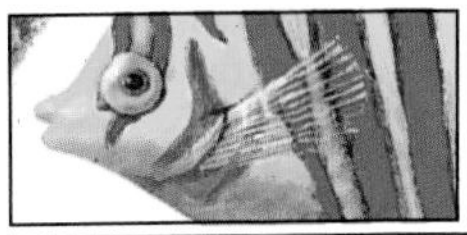

Living Coral

Barrier Islands Formed by Coral—Coral is made up of polyps, sea creatures that live clustered together in warm water with plenty of sunlight. They produce a hard, rocklike material that is actually their skeleton. Year after year, long coral reefs are formed in this way. It takes almost 200 years to create two yards of coral. The largest coral reef in the world is the Great Barrier Reef in Australia.

Habits—Coral cannot move. It lives on the plankton in the water that moves through the reef. Once a year the coral releases eggs that are fertilized as they float to the surface of the water. These fertilized eggs then drop and begin to grow on an existing reef or start a new one.

There are many different varieties of coral. This dark red coral grows in the Mediterranean Sea.

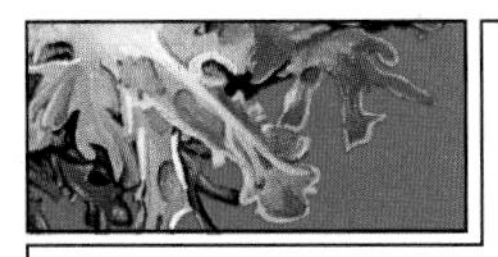

Camouflage

Scorpion Fish—Many animals in the sea have very good camouflage. That means they can look like the surrounding reef or rocks or seaweed, or just like the color of the water. Their enemies often mistake them for part of the background. One fish with very good camouflage is the scorpion fish—a strange fish that spends most of its time lying in the reef where it lives. Its body is hard and covered with poisonous spines that look like rocks encrusted with shells. The scorpion fish can keep so still that small fish swimming right by it mistake it for part of the coral reef. Suddenly the scorpion fish will dart out and capture them.

Under the Sand—Skates live on the ocean floor. They are kite-shaped fish the same color as the sand at the bottom of the sea. They burrow into the sand and their camouflage is so good they are hard to see.

Flat Fish—The sole is almost invisible at the bottom of the sea where it usually stays. Young soles look like ordinary fish, but as they grow they get flatter and flatter. Adult soles are so flat that they have an upper side and a lower side. Eventually, both eyes and its scales are on the upper side.

A Fish as Thin as a Needle—The needlefish hides in seaweed. Soft and wavy as the seaweed in which it hides, the needlefish waits to swallow any small fish that swim by.

Fish and many other animals have adapted so well to their environment that they are almost impossible to see. Soldiers in wartime use camouflage so that the enemy can't see them.

The scorpion fish looks ugly, but its appearance is good camouflage. It is difficult to tell the scorpion fish from its surroundings. Good camouflage is protection against enemies especially while waiting to catch something to eat.

False Fish

Mammals—Whales, sperm whales, grampuses, and dolphins belong to the cetacean order. They look like fish, but they are marine mammals. Their babies nurse and stay with their mothers until they are old enough to look after themselves. They have fins and tails like fish, but like all mammals, they must come out of the water to breathe. Some of these animals can stay under water for as long as an hour. Some marine mammals grow to be very large. A blue whale can grow to more than 100 feet long.

In the Mouth of a Whale—When whales suck in enormous quantities of water, they also take in small crustaceans and plankton, which are their food. Sperm whales and grampuses eat larger prey.

Dolphins—Dolphins communicate with each other by making whistles and very high-pitched sounds that scientists are trying to understand.

1-humpback whale 2-gray whale 3-blue whale 4-porpoise 5-sperm whale 6-narwhals 7-killer whale 8-white dolphin

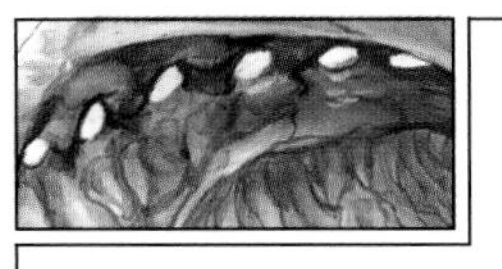

Collecting Shells

Triton shell

Soft Creatures—Many sea creatures have no bones in their bodies. To protect and support themselves, crustaceans such as lobsters, shrimp, and crabs are covered

Chrysanthemum shell

by "armor," a hard crust that is actually an external skeleton. Mollusks such as oysters and mussels create shells, little homes in which they live and are protected. The shell grows as the animal that lives inside it grows.

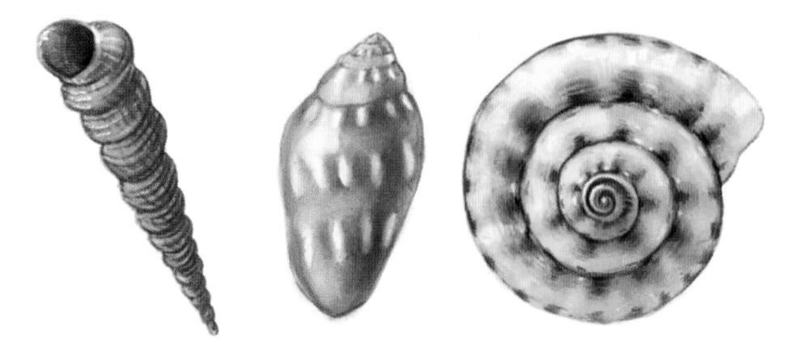
Turritella shell Wenteltrap Sundial shell

Two Kinds—There are shells formed as a single piece in a spiral or other simple shape. These are called "univalves." Shells made up of two halves are called "bivalves."

Life of a Mollusk—Many mollusks spend their entire lives anchored firmly to a rock. Others hide under the sand and only come out at high tide to take in the nutrients in seawater. Still others move around and swim in the water.

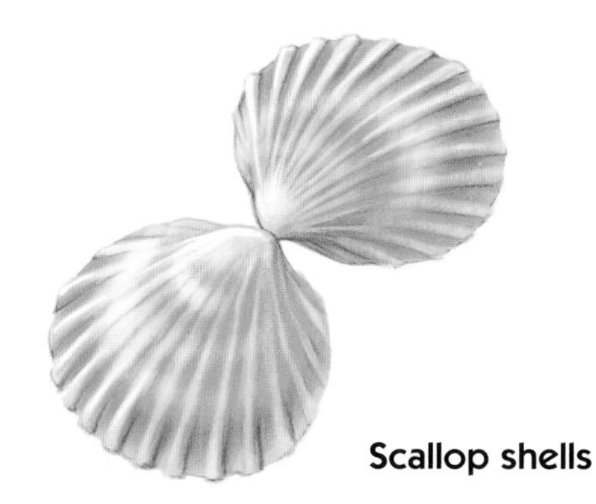
Scallop shells

Shell-Covered Beaches—On some islands the sand is very white, or pinkish.

Giant clam

This is because it is made up of minuscule pieces of shells that have been broken by rocks and smoothed by the sea.

Enormous Mollusks—There are enormous mollusks that live deep in the sea. Some are as big as dinner plates.

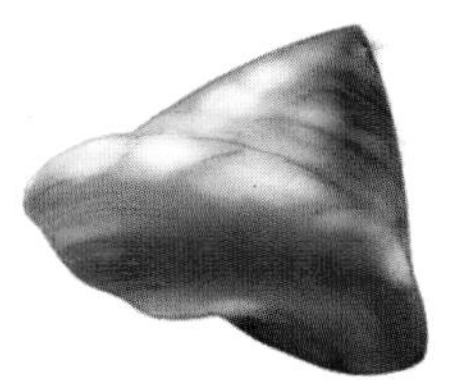

Callistome shell

Cowrie shell

Abalone shell

Miter shell

Cone shell

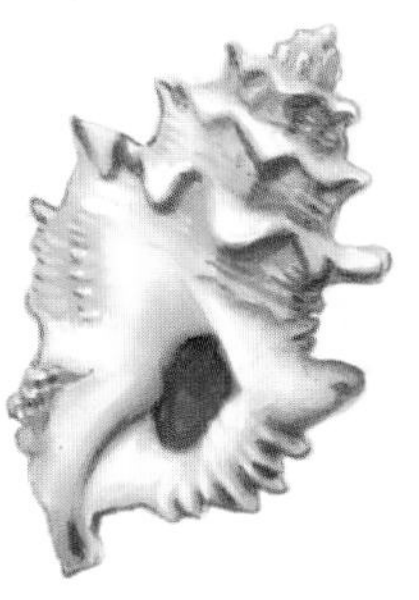

Verco shell

Delicate Flavor—Many shells like clams, mussels, and oysters are delicious to eat. They are raised in great closed-in basins along seacoasts.

History of a Fossil—Millions of years ago a conch shell rested on the ocean floor where it was covered by layers of sand and mud. As time passed the waters drew back and the bottom, now a rocky crust, emerged. The shell remained trapped in the rocks and eventually broke into bits. The imprint of the conch shell in the rock is called a "fossil." This fossil imprint is still perfectly visible today. Fossils are often found on mountains that millions of years ago made up the ocean floor.

Murex shell

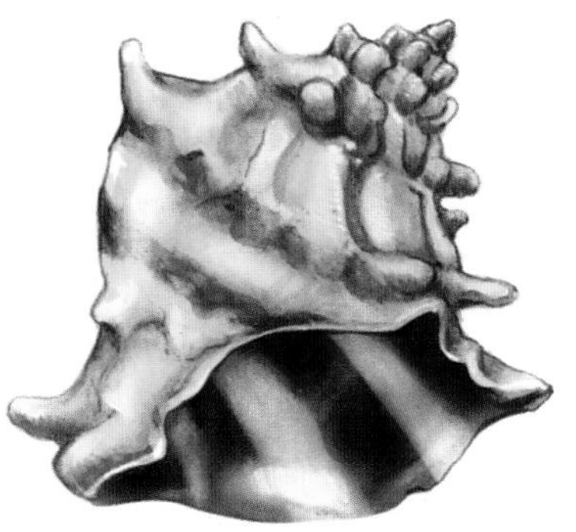

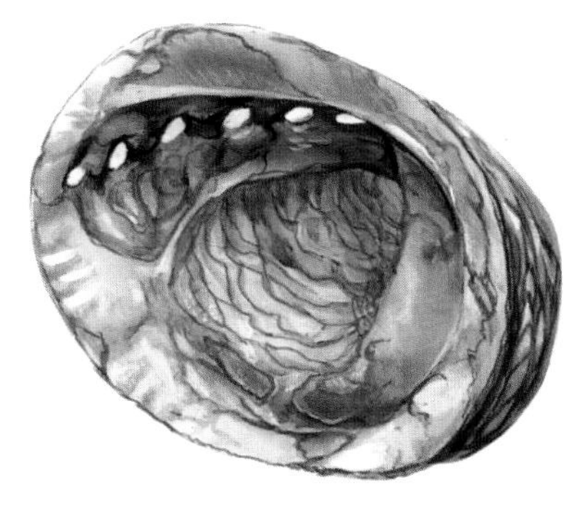

Cone shell

How to Collect Shells—You can start your own shell collection by just walking along a beach and gathering some. Make sure you pick up empty shells that don't have anything living in them. When you get home, rinse the shells in fresh water and let them dry. Glue them to card-board with white glue. With the help of a book, you can identify them and write their English or Latin name beneath each one.

Nautilus shell

Pearls and Corals

The most precious pearls are those that are perfectly round and have no imperfections.

Mother of Pearl—Shirt buttons are often made of mother of pearl, the substance that covers the inside of some shells.

Pearls—When a grain of sand gets inside an oyster shell, the oyster produces a substance called "nacre" which covers the sand and forms a pearl. Not all oysters contain a pearl—only those that had to protect themselves from foreign matter in their shells.

Precious—Pearls spontaneously grown inside an oyster shell are very rare, and gathering them is very dangerous work because the divers go as deep as 40 feet without oxygen tanks. At one time that was the only way to get pearls. Today there are oyster farms where pearls are produced artificially. A small bead is inserted into each oyster shell and the mollusk then covers it with nacre. Pearls that are produced in this way are called "cultured" pearls and are not as precious as those the oysters grow on their own.

Coral—Since ancient times coral has been worn as jewelry and carved to make precious ornaments. The most valuable corals are dark red and clear pink. Coral all over the world is endangered and people should no longer buy it. Some people believe that coral brings good luck.

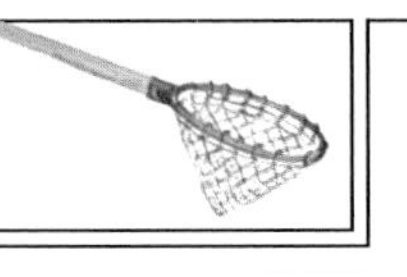

An Aquarium

Friends with Fins—A little goldfish in a bowl has very few needs: fresh water, a clean bowl, a little fish food, and the right light.

Aquariums—Setting up an aquarium, especially a saltwater aquarium, requires much more care. You need to recreate your fish's natural environment. The temperature must be exactly right. The water must constantly have air bubbles pumped into it and the floor of the aquarium must look as much as possible like the natural home that the fish used to live in.

1

2

3

Fish Have Friends and Enemies—There are fish that cannot live together in the same fish tank because they will eat each other. If fish are too crowded, even fish of the same kind will start eating each other. Each fish must have a certain amount of space. Also remember when you set up an aquarium that you cannot mix fresh-water and saltwater fish. Each needs its own environment.

In this picture fresh-water and saltwater fish are shown together, just so you can see what they look like.

1-spadefish 2-carp 3-swordtail
4-black spadefish 5 and 6-Siamese fighting fish
7-seahorse 8-murex shell

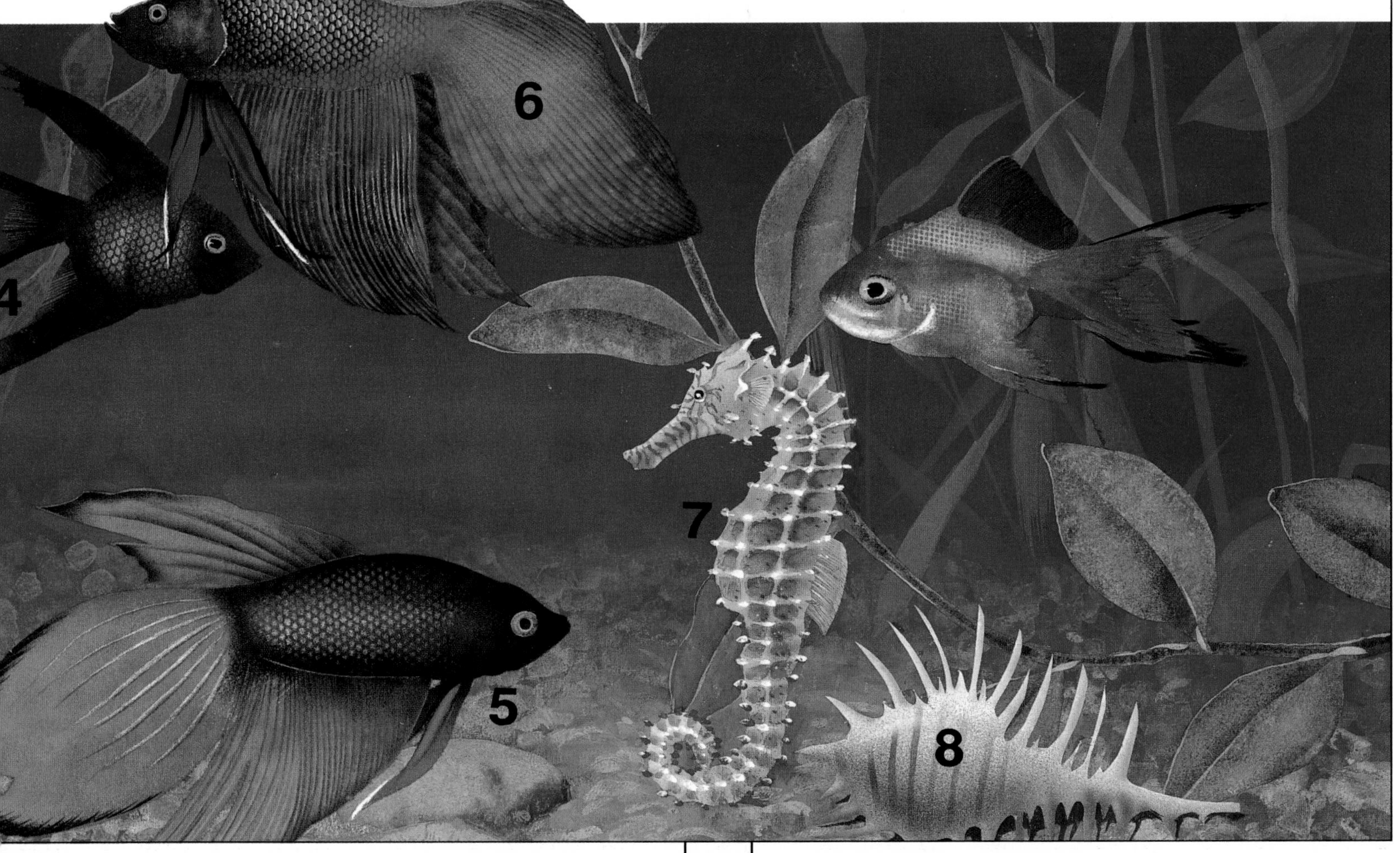

The Sea Is Their Home

The Sea Turtle—This reptile is as ancient as the dinosaurs. It sticks its head out of the water to take a breath of air and then dives down again because it lives in the sea. The female sea turtle leaves the water to lay her eggs on shore. She hides them in the warm sand on the beach, not far from the water. As soon as the baby turtles hatch they make their way to the sea, but they are in great danger from the seagulls and large crabs that eat them.

Always Near the Sea—Many animals that live on land depend on the sea. Seals, walruses, sea lions, and penguins live on ice, rocks, or the beaches at the edge of the sea. Many birds like seagulls, albatrosses, and stormy petrels also live along the seashores and in the rocky crags along coastlines. They are all marine animals.

Plankton—Billions and billions of minute sea organisms form plankton, the favorite food of whales. It is also a necessary nutrient for many fishes.